A New Roof

DISCARD

Written by Cari Meister   Illustrated by Grace Lin

Children's Press®
A Division of Scholastic Inc.
New York • Toronto • London • Auckland • Sydney
Mexico City • New Delhi • Hong Kong
Danbury, Connecticut

For the guys at Incline Roofing
—C.M.

Reading Consultants

Linda Cornwell
Literacy Specialist

Katharine A. Kane
Education Consultant
(Retired, San Diego County Office of Education
and San Diego State University)

Library of Congress Cataloging-in-Publication Data

Meister, Cari.
    A new roof / written by Cari Meister ; illustrated by Grace Lin.
        p. cm. – (Rookie reader)
    Summary: A boy's roof is leaking, and he watches the process as a crew
of workers come to fix it.
    ISBN 0-516-22369-0 (lib. bdg.) 0-516-27382-5 (pbk.)
    [1. Roofing—Fiction.] I. Lin, Grace, ill. II. Title. III. Series.
PZ7.M515916 Ne 2002
[E]—dc21   2001003835

A drip. A drop.
A drop. A drip.

3

We need a new roof!

A truck.
Some workers.
Climb the ladder.

A shovel.
A pick.
Lots of clatter!

9

Rip. Rip. Rip.
Tear. Tear. Tear.
Look out below!

New shingles.
New nails.
Up the ladder.

13

Some water.
A snack.
Then they hammer.

Pound. Pound. Pound.
Pound! Pound! Pound!

All done!

19

No more drips.
No more drops.

A new roof!

Word List (38 words)

a	hammer	out	the
all	ladder	pick	then
below	look	pound	they
clatter	lots	rip	truck
climb	more	roof	up
done	nails	shingles	water
drip	need	shovel	we
drips	new	snack	workers
drop	no	some	
drops	of	tear	

About the Author

Cari Meister lives on a small farm in Minnesota with her husband John, her son Edwin, their dog Samson, two horses, three cats, two pigs, and two goats. She is the author of more than twenty books for children, including *I Love Rocks, Catch That Cat,* and *Game Day* in the Rookie Reader series.

About the Illustrator

Grace Lin grew up in upstate New York and went to the Rhode Island School of Design. She is the author and illustrator of the books *The Ugly Vegetables* and *Dim Sum for Everyone!* Since Grace will be moving soon, she, too, will have a new roof.